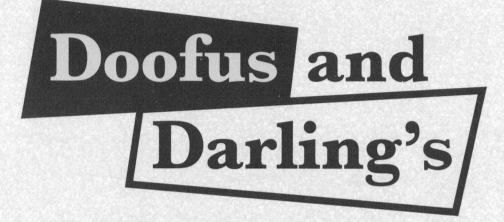

Doofus and Darling's

MANNERS FOR THE MODERN MAN

Doofus and Darling's

MANNERS FOR THE MODERN MAN

A Handy Guide for Today's Ambiguous Etiquette Situations

David Hoffman

Foreword by Faith Salie
Illustrations by Mark Zingarelli

BLACK DOG
& LEVENTHAL
PUBLISHERS
NEW YORK

A QUIRK PACKAGING BOOK

Published by
BLACK DOG & LEVENTHAL PUBLISHERS, INC.
151 West 19th Street
New York, NY 10011
www.blackdogandleventhal.com

Distributed by
WORKMAN PUBLISHING COMPANY
225 Varick Street
New York, NY 10014

Manufactured in the United States of America

Cover and interior design by Lynne Yeamans/Quirk Packaging, Inc.
Illustrations by Mark Zingarelli

ISBN-13: 978-1-57912-793-0

h g f e d c b a

Library of Congress Cataloging-in-Publication Data is on file at Black Dog & Leventhal Publishers, Inc.

Purchasing this book indicates that you have an excellent sense of humor.
However, on the off-chance that you are 1) very literal 2) entirely unaware of popular children's
culture or 3) feeling cranky at the moment, we want to make absolutely, positively certain that you
realize **THIS BOOK IS A PARODY** and has not been prepared, approved, or authorized by
the creators or producers of *Highlights® for Children* or "Goofus and Gallant®." It's pure silliness,
just for fun, and not intended to educate or enlighten in any way. So please just enjoy it—and don't
sue anybody!

To Mom, and also my sister Susie—not to mention the countless other women* who, over the years, at one time or another, in one way or another, have worked to turn this Doofus into a Darling

*Joyce Agee, Lisa Allen, Martha Anderson, Diane Asselin Baer, Patti Breitman, Judi Casey, Andrea Marquit Clagett, Dean Bear, Susan Duncan, Donna Forman, Cathie Galvin, Mary Pat Gleason, Laurie Jacoby, Barbara Karlin, Leah Komaiko, Mollie MacDonald, Irene Mecchi, Jill Mullikin-Bates, Wanda Parton, Jan Pomerantz, Lynn Powers, Dale Raoul, Margot Ravon, Laurie Sale, Susie Saunders, Bird Smith, Snookie Stoddard, Lisa Trachtman, Brenda Wilson, and Leslie Zerg

Contents

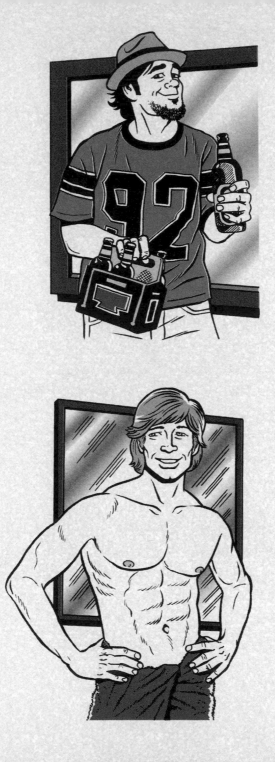

Foreword

Where was *Doofus and Darling's Manners for the Modern Man* when that guy I was seeing took me to Honolulu for New Year's Eve...and we rang in midnight at Hooters? Or when I was on an idyllically romantic date in Barcelona, and my dream man studied my candlelit face and asked, "Have you ever broken your nose?" And where was it when my erstwhile Doofus accidentally showed my parents a videotape of him having sex with a hot blond?*

Ah, well, better late than never. *Doofus and Darling's Manners for the Modern Man* is a gift to all man and womankind. I encourage frustrated and flummoxed women everywhere to give a dude this book. I suspect its excellent ratio of pictures to words will be more effective than saying, "Seriously, did you not have a *mother*?!"

Though the old adage says, "A picture is worth a thousand words," sometimes you only want a picture to convey simple things: "Please don't say I have 'birthing hips'"; "A scale is not a proper Valentine's Day present"; and, "Actually, it's *not* funny to fart and say, 'Look out for the barking spider!'"

But let me be clear, not every man needs this book. My father and my brothers don't. Jesus probably didn't. I think that might be it.

This is not an etiquette primer with antediluvian questions like, "Which fork do I use?" (outside in, duh), or, "Do I always have to open the door for my lady?" (yes, please). No, this is a timely, relevant guide made all the more accessible by depicting Doofus—at his worst—looking like Benicio Del Toro on a bender and Darling—at his best—looking like a somewhat gay version of Brad Pitt (which is really every woman's dream man, no?).

But don't be distracted by its sparkly humor; this guide is a public service—and in some cases, a pubic service (see pages 34-35 devoted to "On Good Grooming").

Manners do matter. Good behavior demonstrates respect, compassion, and gratitude. And just ask a Darling: good manners get you laid.

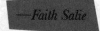

—*Faith Salie*

The hot blond was not me, which was a good thing...I think.

Introduction

I blame it all on my parents.

I was born in Richmond, Virginia, where manners rank in importance with barbecue, the Civil War, and your mother's maiden name. The first words out of my mouth were probably "excuse me," unless I'm forgetting that I had already said "thank you" to the doctor who guided the delivery. Although my folks were, what I would call, "conservatively cool" (it was okay for me to use a four-letter word in the house; just not okay if I was using it in reference to *them*), they definitely had strong opinions on how their kids (and people in general) should behave. Being polite has served me well...well, except in my late teens, when inevitably the mothers of the girls I dated liked me more than they did. I am the product of a mom who could have taught Emily Post a thing or two about how to write a thank you note (and who taught me how to write creatively in the process) and of a dad, who for twenty-five years after he quit smoking, continued to carry a lighter in his jacket pocket so that he could light my mother's cigarettes.

Manners matter to me.

That's not to say that I always remember to use them.

I admit that on occasion I have been less appreciative of a gift than I should have been. But please, it was a *blouse* not a shirt...

I acknowledge that I think nothing of grabbing food off someone else's plate, although I do understand—even if I do use a fork—why this might be construed as impolite.

I own up to secretly watching television while talking on the phone, and then, when caught not really listening, blaming the distraction on bad reception ("...you're breaking up!")—or on a non-existent truck or bus outside my window.

And I agree that the most mature way to react to the guy, who (on the Saturday before Christmas in one of the most congested shopping areas in Los Angeles) flipped a U-turn, cut me off, and stole the parking space I was about to pull into, probably wasn't by attempting to let the air out of his tires.

Apparently, I am not alone.

Today, studies show that people are more ill-mannered than ever; we're rude, crude, and full of 'tude. If it's not road rage, airport rage, desk rage, checkout rage, or check-in rage, then it's sideline rage, cell phone rage, theater rage, smoking rage, pet poop rage, car alarm rage...

Is it me, or was there simply more emphasis on civility when I was growing up? Born in the '50s, raised in the '60s, and educated in the '70s, it seems that everywhere I turned, no matter how old I got, I got a lesson in etiquette. Besides the grandmother who would bribe me to use good table manners (unfortunately for her, I stopped falling for it once I discovered that she was paying my older brother and sister more than she was paying me) and books by Munro Leaf (*How to Behave and Why* and *Manners Can Be Fun*), we had the *Romper Room* Do-Bee ("I always do everything right/I never do anything wrong/I'm a Romper Room Do Bee/A Do Bee all day long!"), cotillion, sage advice from "Ann Landers" and "Dear Abby," and an endless stream of in-school "social guidance" films*—those 16mm classroom movies with titles such as "Dating: Do's and Don'ts," "Body Care and Grooming," "Are You Popular?" and "Let's Play Safe" (although that one centered on the spread of communism and concern over the atomic bomb and had nothing to do with using a condom).

But one of my most treasured childhood learning experiences arrived at the beginning of every month, measured just over 8½ x 11 inches, and promised "Fun With a Purpose." *Highlights® for Children*—a staple of pediatricians' waiting rooms and school libraries nationwide—had such an impact on me (not to mention the generations that have followed) that the mere mention of the magazine immediately conjures up shared conversations about "Hidden Pictures," "The Timbertoes," and "Goofus and Gallant."

"Goofus and Gallant" was a dual panel "comic strip" (in illustration terms only; as written, it was never intended to be funny) in which a set of twins (or were they, in fact, the same person existing in parallel universes?) offered up

---

*Attention trivia lovers: *A large number of these films were bankrolled by John Wayne, whose stand-in Sid Davis created and directed almost three dozen of them.*

examples of right and wrong. Goofus, who was drawn with messy hair and a bratty grin on his face, was loud, ill-behaved, and inconsiderate ("Goofus doesn't tell the sales clerk when she fails to charge him for every item in his order"). Gallant, by contrast, was perfectly groomed, well-mannered, and a model citizen ("Gallant points out that he purchased two comic books but that he was only charged for one").

I hadn't thought about *Highlights* in quite some time until I accidentally spied a copy of the magazine at the home of my friend Susie, a kindergarten teacher. My initial response when I picked it up was to do what I had done so many years before: flip it open, thumb through the table of contents, and go immediately to the latest installment of "Goofus and Gallant."

I wasn't surprised that they were there, (FYI, sixty-plus years after it was first introduced, *Highlights* still has more subscribers than any other general interest magazine for kids) but I chuckled to myself as I read the mini-morality lesson, noting that little had changed. Goofus skipping choir practice to watch something on television, and Gallant keeping his commitment to attending a team meeting because he had given his word that he would be there, were as much 1958 as they were 2008. And then it hit. We'd all grown up with Goofus and Gallant—and we knew how we turned out. But I wondered, instead of staying perpetually twelve or thirteen years old, what if they had grown up as well...what would have happened to them? And what social skills sets would they be teaching us now?

Enter *Doofus and Darling's Manners for the Modern Man*, a modern primer for today's man that leaves no toilet seat up in examining the do's and don'ts of contemporary etiquette situations.

—*David Hoffman*

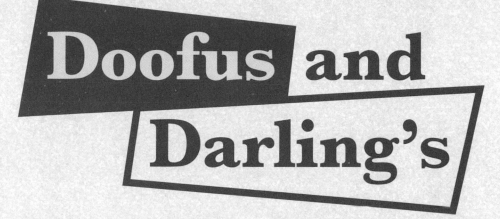

GALLERY OF DO'S AND DON'TS

Doofus checks his BlackBerry® every ten minutes during dinner.

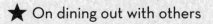

★ On dining out with others

Darling believes that, unless he is an on-call brain surgeon,
the only hand-held device appropriate for restaurant use is a fork.

Doofus hogs the remote control and can only watch
television if he is changing the channel every other second.

★ On watching television

Darling is not only able to relax and enjoy watching television when someone else controls the remote—he can do so even if the set is tuned to a marathon of Lifetime Channel original movies.

Doofus pees all over the toilet bowl,
instead of peeing *in* it.

★ On cultivating responsible bathroom behavior

Darling aims carefully while peeing, wipes off the rim should he miss, and always puts the seat back down when he is done.

Doofus does not hide his disappointment and lets it be known when he receives a gift he does not like.

★ On appreciation of others' kindnesses

Darling is thankful for any present he receives, even if it is boring or butt-ugly, as he appreciates the thought—and because he knows that there is always someone to whom he can re-gift it.

Doofus monologues.

 On showing a genuine interest in others

Darling dialogues.

Doofus spreads rumors and stirs the pot.

★ On suitable versus unsuitable social interactions

Darling does rumor control—and stirs the perfect martini.

Doofus does not bother to think twice before asking,
"When are you due?"

★ On choosing one's words carefully

Darling never comments on a woman being pregnant
unless he personally sees the sonogram.

Doofus thinks flatulence is funny.

★ On having a good sense of humor

Darling thinks Tina Fey is funny.

Doofus laughs when he sees someone embarrass themselves in public, and captures their misfortune on his camera phone so that he can later post it on YouTube®.

★ On easing others' embarrassment

Darling knows when to pretend that he did not see
someone embarrass themselves—and when to step in
and offer some assistance.

Doofus would solve the dilemma of losing his hair
with a comb-over.

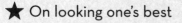 On looking one's best

Darling would embrace his male pattern baldness
by rocking a receding hairline.

Doofus does not realize that he is supposed to have two distinct eyebrows and that hair care should not stop at the neck.

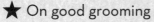 On good grooming

Darling manscapes (carefully).

Doofus's idea of daily exercise is popping open a six-pack.

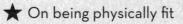 On being physically fit

Darling has a six-pack.

Doofus refuses to turn off his cell phone when
he is at the theater—and answers it when it rings.

 On proper theater-going behavior

Darling turns off his phone before he even arrives
at the theater, knowing that others are there to hear
the performance, not to listen to his ringtone.

Doofus is inconsiderate of his fellow passengers and focuses only on making himself comfortable.

★ On respecting others' personal space

Darling always offers to take the center seat.

Doofus does not bother to scoop after his pooch poops.

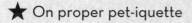 On proper pet-iquette

Darling always stops to clean up—even when it was not his dog.

Doofus orders cocktails before dinner,
wine with the meal, and an aperitif after dessert—
then suggests that everyone split the bill.

★ On the importance of learning good math skills

Darling slips the waiter his credit card before dinner,
and informs him that he plans to pick up the bill.

Doofus uses an elderly relative's handicap placard
so that he can get the best parking space.

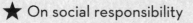 On social responsibility

Darling drives a hybrid or alternative-fuel vehicle
in order to get preferential parking.

Doofus honks his horn and gestures to other drivers with a wave of the middle finger.

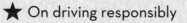 On driving responsibly

Darling sits in traffic patiently and gestures
with a courteous wave.

Doofus throws a tantrum when he loses,
and stomps away, fuming.

★ On learning good sportsmanship
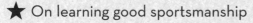

Darling loses graciously, offering his congratulations
to those who have beaten him.

Doofus presents others' ideas as his own,
and has no qualms taking all the credit.

★ On learning good work habits

Darling presents his project as a collaborative effort, points out everyone else's contributions, and purposely schedules new ideas meetings for noon so that the company brings in lunch.

Doofus picks up a woman this way.

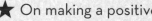 On making a positive first impression

Darling picks up a woman this way.

Doofus asks, "Are those real?"

★ On getting to know someone better

Darling looks a woman in the eye when he is talking to her,
making her feel like she is the only person in the room.

Doofus hits on women at funerals, extending his hand and slipping the widow his phone number.

★ On knowing there's a time and place for everything

Darling extends his hand to everyone at funerals,
but only to offer his condolences.

Doofus lies about his age and relationship status
in his online profile.

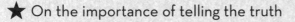 On the importance of telling the truth

Darling does not care that his online interest
fudged her stats in her dating profile.

Doofus brags about how much money he makes
and the cost of everything he owns.

★ On knowing the value of things

Darling never mentions dollar amounts unless he
is phoning in a pledge to a charity telethon.

Doofus calls everybody "dude."

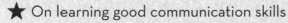 ★ On learning good communication skills

Darling remembers to call his mother.

Doofus sets the mood for a night of lovemaking
by bookmarking Internet porn.

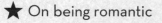 On being romantic

Darling sets the mood with a book of sonnets,
candles, rose petals, and a foot rub.

How Doofus attends a sporting event

★ On making sure your guests are having a good time

How Darling attends a sporting event

Doofus always ends his dates with "three little words," even if he does not mean them.

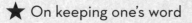

★ On keeping one's word

Darling says "I'll call you"—and does.

Doofus says, "Let me put it this way:
No way in hell am I going to see that movie."

★ On respecting differences

Darling says, "It's nice we can see this movie together."

Doofus is only concerned with satisfying himself
and falls asleep as soon as he is done.

★ On self-control and the lack of it

Darling makes sure that "it was good for you, too" — and only gets out of bed to cook breakfast the next morning.

Doofus throws his condom wrappers on the floor.

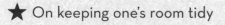 On keeping one's room tidy

Darling picks up his condom wrappers, puts them in the wastebasket, and then, as long as he is at it, empties the trash.

Doofus lets his girlfriend know he wants to break up by changing his Facebook® status from "in a relationship" to "single."

★ On expressing one's feelings

Darling breaks up face to face, does it with honesty,
and never in a public place.

Doofus brags about the family jewels.

Darling buys his wife or girlfriend jewelry.

Doofus acts like a kid.

 On age-appropriate behavior

Darling wants to have kids.

Doofus opens the refrigerator and asks,
"What's for dinner?"

 On thoughtful behavior

Darling opens the refrigerator and announces
what he will be making for dinner.

Doofus asks, "Are you sure you need that?"

 On appropriate versus inappropriate comments

Darling asks, "Don't you need some ice cream with that?"

Doofus considers the dishes done when he has
licked his plate clean.

★ On sharing household chores

Darling says, "Here, let me do the dishes. You must be tired."

Doofus sits at the breakfast table with his head buried in the sports section of the paper.

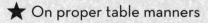 On proper table manners

Darling shares the day's headlines, selflessly gives up
the crossword, and points out an ad for a Manolo Blahnik®
sale while he reads the paper.

Doofus says, "I think what you're wearing is fine. I thought what you had on five minutes ago was fine, too. I'm sure if you wear something else, that will look fine. Can we just go now?"

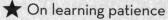 On learning patience

Darling says, "Take as long as you need to get ready, honey. I don't mind waiting one bit."

Doofus believes he actually looks good in a Speedo®.

★ On knowing what (not) to wear

Darling has no problem wearing whatever it is his wife
or girlfriend asks him to wear, even if it is pink.

Doofus catches a minor cold and demands to be brought soup and freshly squeezed juice—not to mention herbal tea, menthol rub, a cool-mist humidifier, a warm foot bath, cough drops, and nasal spray—while he whines and stays in bed all day.

★ On proper sickbed behavior

Darling asks for nothing when he is sick, except that
he be left alone—and takes his cold into the guest room
so he does not spread his germs.

Doofus does not remember birthdays, but he remembers the box scores from every major league baseball game since 1957, knows the name of every model who has appeared in the swimsuit edition of *Sports Illustrated*, and can recite the dialogue from *Tommy Boy*, scene by scene, line by line.

★ On remembering what's important

Darling remembers birthdays and anniversaries—
and also remembers it doesn't have to be one of those
days in order for him to show up with flowers.

Doofus fails to notice when his wife or girlfriend cuts her hair, has on a new outfit, or redecorates the house.

★ On developing observational skills

Darling not only notices when things are different, but he
also offers styling tips on the new haircut, suggests the
perfect shoes and bag to go with the new outfit, and figures
out the best way to arrange the new furnishings.

Doofus hires a new assistant with a 38-inch chest.

★ On making smart business decisions

Darling hires a new assistant with 38 years' experience.

Doofus hears his mother-in-law is coming to visit and immediately makes plans to spend the weekend in Vegas with the guys.

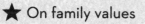 On family values

Darling hears his mother-in-law is coming to visit
and is disappointed that she is staying for only the weekend
and not the entire week.

Doofus insists on being Mr. Fix-It around the house,
even though this will cost him twice as much when the
repair service has to come anyway.

★ On learning when to ask for help

Darling calls the repair service immediately, and with
the money he saves by not trying to do the work himself,
buys two tickets to Hawaii.

Doofus complains that he has trouble sleeping
with the light on when his wife gets up in the middle
of the night to feed the baby.

★ On cultivating responsible parenting behavior

Darling insists that his wife stay in bed and *he* be
the one to get up and handle the baby's nighttime feedings.

Doofus does not think twice about buying a brand new two-seater convertible—even though he now has kids.

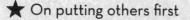 On putting others first